Co

L

Che

Publishing Ltd

www.countrysidedogwalks.co.uk

First published in April 2016 by **Wet Nose Publishing Ltd**
All enquiries regarding sales telephone: 01824 704398
email cdw@wetnosepublishing.co.uk
www.countrysidedogwalks.co.uk
ISBN 978-0-9931923-3-3

We would like to express our gratitude to Steve Goodier for researching many of the walks within this publication.

We would also like to thank Steve Thorley for proof-reading this edition.

Liverpool

Manchester

Cheshire

Warrington

1

3
4
2   5   Wlimslow   6   7

Frodsham

Knutsford

8
9
10

Macclesfield

14   11
13   12
15 Winsford

Chester

Cheshire

Congleton   18
16
17

20
19

Malpas

Contents

Introduction 1

1. Risley Moss (Easy)..7

2. Tatton Hall (Easy)...11

3. Quarry Bank (Easy)...15

4. Southern Woods (Easy)..19

5. Lindow Common (Medium)..23

6. Ladybrook Valley (Easy)...27

7. Lyme Park (Medium)..31

8. Marbury Park (Easy)..35

9. Neumann's Flash (Medium)...39

10. Anderton Nature Reserve (Medium)...43

11. Tegg's Nose (Challenging)..47

12. Macclesfield Forest (Challenging)..53

13. Delamere Old Pale (Medium)...57

14. Delamere Blakemere Moss (Easy)..61

15. The Kennels (Easy)..65

16. Brereton Heath Mere (Easy)..69

17. Astbury Mere (Easy)..73

18. The Cloud (Medium/Challenging)...77

19. Raw Head (Medium)..81

20. Beeston (Medium/Challenging)..85

Introduction

The twenty walks included in this book are all designed so that you and your wet-nosed friend have a really enjoyable time. Where there are stiles, they are specially designed with lift gates for dogs. At a quick glance, there is information at the beginning of each walk to tell you what to expect and what you may need to take with you. The descriptive guides will also warn of any roads ahead or areas of livestock so that you can get your dog on the lead well in advance.

Dogs just love to explore new places. They really enjoy the new smells and carry themselves a little higher with the added excitement. Going to new places gets you and your dog out and about, meeting new people and their dogs. It is important to socialise dogs, as they will be more likely to act in a friendly manner towards other dogs as they gain confidence.

The stunning pictures in this book are just a taster of what you can see along the way. Many of the walks have fantastic views and scenery. Some of the walks are wooded, offering shade on those hot summer days.

The walks are graded Easy, Medium and Challenging. They are all around one to three hours long, depending on your and your dog's pace. You may start with the easy ones and work up to the challenging walks depending on your and your dog's fitness. Different dog breeds and dog age must be taken into account when you decide which walks to do.

Different breeds of dog have different levels of fitness. For example, bulldogs

can only do short walks whereas a border collie or a springer spaniel are extremely energetic and difficult to tire out. It is recommended that you do some research on the breed of dog that you own to get to know what sort of exercise that they require.

You may have a walk that you are happy doing with your dog every day, but this book will show you new areas to explore with a change of scenery and a chance to meet new people and their dogs. Dogs love new places to visit and you will see the change in them as they explore the new surroundings, taking in the new smells with delight. You will fulfil both your life and your dog's just by trying somewhere new.

Some of the walks include bridleways, so you may encounter horses and cyclists. It is important to put your dog on a lead if you see horses approach. It is always helpful to say hello to the riders as they near, so that the horse realises that you are not a threat.

Ground Nesting Birds

Watch out for vulnerable ground nesting birds during 1st of March until the end of July. Dogs that stray off the main paths may disturb birds and chicks, possibly killing them or breaking eggs. Species to look out for are Sky larks, Meadow pipits, Curlew, Red and Black grouse, Snipe and Pheasants.

Some if not all of these birds are declining in numbers, due partly to their vulnerability when nesting. Dogs are a threat to them, even by treading on them unintentionally. Some other threats are foxes, badgers, stoats, weasels, birds of prey and crows.

Please help to protect these birds during the nesting season by keeping your dog on the paths when walking in open areas such as grassland, moors, heathland and scrub.

Rivers

Some dogs love water and will think nothing of plunging into the river. With the extreme weather conditions over the last few years, a river that may be safe for your dog to swim in can change in a matter of hours to become a swollen torrent that could wash your dog away. Please be careful when near rivers if there have been heavy periods of rain or if they look swollen or fast flowing. It is best to put your dogs on the lead, until you have assessed the situation.

Livestock

If you find that you need to cross a field with cattle or horses and they seem interested in you or your dog, it is recommended within the Countryside Code to let your dog off the lead. Never try to get between livestock and your dog. Your dog will get out of a situation a lot more easily with speed than you can. It is usually only cattle with young calves that are a threat, or young heifers or bullocks that tend to get a little inquisitive. They will usually stop when they get close to you or your dog.

Most horses will come over for a fuss but a small proportion do have a problem with dogs. They may see them as a threat and will act to defend the herd. Horses that are out with a rider are completely different as they are not defending the herd, and as long as you keep a safe distance there should not be a problem.

Sheep are not a danger to you, but your dog can be a danger to them. Where sheep are grazing it is vital that you have your dog on a lead or under very close control. You will know your dog, but if you are unsure it is better to play safe and keep your dog on a lead. It is important always to have your dog on a lead when around lambs. Lambs have a higher pitched bleat and can be the size of a cat, and your dog may act differently amongst them.

Ticks

If you have been walking in areas where sheep graze you should check your dog, for ticks. They must be removed as soon as possible. It is best to use tick tweezers, which are specially designed to remove the head and leg parts of the tick. Ticks can carry diseases and the longer they remain latched on to your dog the more the chance of spreading infections.

Forests

The forest walks in this book are a changing landscape, which makes them unique and interesting. Descriptions may change with time, for instance a path may be described as being in the shade of the forest, but as this is a worked forest a section could be clear felled at any time. Another change over the years could be where a view is described across a previously felled area. This could then be planted up with trees growing up to block the views. Paths may change but this is less likely. On rare occasions the Forestry Commission may temporarily close paths due to forest works but again this is even less likely on a weekend. Any changes to the path networks that may occur after the date of print will be updated on our website.

Does your dog fetch a stick?

Most dogs love sticks and will pick them up without any encouragement from their owners. Vets and dog trainers recommend that you should not throw sticks for dogs. They can cause nasty injuries, sometimes fatal as the stick can pierce the throat, or rebound off the ground and cause harm to your dog.

Please clean up after your dog

Always be prepared, having dog bags with you at all times. Once you have cleaned up after your dog, please keep the bag, until you see a bin. If there are no bins provided, then take it away with you to a roadside bin. Dog bags that are discarded on the paths or in the bushes are unpleasant and unsightly and will not degrade.

1. Risley Moss

Easy - 1.3 miles - 1hr

This is a wonderful short circular walk through mixed woodland, where in areas silver birch dominate. There is a wooden tower, from which you will have wonderful views across the moss, which is a greatly declining habitat. The paths are surfaced except for a short section beside a small area of moss. There are some steps on this walk, but if you have an old dog these can easily be avoided. As this is a nature reserve, please keep your dog under close control. The rangers ask that you keep your dog out of the ponds, as these are important breeding areas for the rare great crested newt.

How to get there – From junction 11 off the M62, follow signs for Warrington and Risley on the A574. At the roundabout turn left, following the brown sign for Risley Moss. Continue to follow the brown signs until you reach the nature reserve.

Grid Reference – SJ 664921

Postcode – WA3 6QS

Parking – Free in the car park

Facilities – There are toilets in the visitor centre

You will need – Dog lead, poop bags

Countryside Dog Walks - Cheshire

The Walk

1 To start the walk, face the main entrance for the visitor centre and turn left. Almost immediately turn right, and just after, turn left. Continue around a right hand bend on the wide surfaced path, where you continue through the mixed broadleaved wood. You will pass a pond on your left. As you continue, you will reach a fingerpost. Turn left and continue around a right hand bend. You will reach the wooden tower, which is worth the climb up the steps, as you will be rewarded with amazing views across the large open moss.

2 Retrace your steps back to the main path and turn left. You will pass another pond on your left. You will pass a hide on your right. Continue on the path, where you will pass an area of rhododendrons, which dominate the woodland floor. Pass a path on your right and continue straight ahead, following the sign on the fingerpost for Mossland Hide. Silver birch dominates the woodland here.

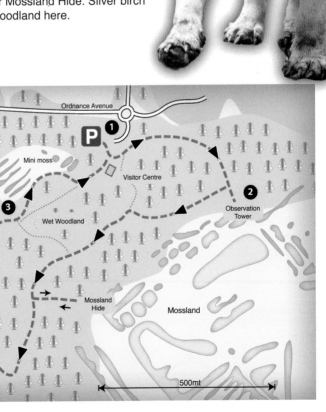

Pass another fingerpost on your left and a path on your right. The area on your left is woodland carr/wet woodland. Continue straight ahead and on reaching another fingerpost you have the option of turning left to view the moss once again, from a bird hide. Or simply continue straight ahead. Pass a pond on your left and shortly after, turn round a sharp right hand bend, where you will pass a pond on your right.

Continue on the main path, where you will pass some open grass areas. You will pass wooden sculptures and an entrance into an open picnic area on your left.

❸ Immediately after, turn left on the path, which is signed on the fingerpost for Mini Moss. Cross the sleeper bridge over a ditch, where you can view the moss on your left. At the end of the path, ascend the steps and turn left on the main path. You will soon reach back to the visitor centre.

2. Tatton Hall

Easy - 2.6 miles - 1hr 30min

This circular walk is in the estate grounds of Tatton Hall, where red and fallow deer roam, therefore you will need to keep your dog under close control or on a lead at all times. There are parkland trees amongst the grassland and some woodland blocks. You will also walk beside a large pond/lake for part of the walk. Most of the paths are fairly flat on this walk. There are no roads. Please note – Tatton Park is closed on Mondays during the winter months; please check the website for more details - www.tattonpark.org.uk

How to get there - Tatton Park is signposted from the M56. Exit at junction 7 and continue to follow the brown signs for Tatton Park, which is roughly a ten minute drive from the motorway.

Postcode – WA16 6QN

Grid Reference – SJ 41816

Parking – Pay on entrance

Facilities – There are toilets, a café and a visitor centre

You will need – Dog leads, dog bags

The Walk

❶ On leaving your car, walk in the opposite direction of the entrance to your parking bay. You will reach a tarmac path. Turn left. On reaching a welcome sign and a map, turn right. As you continue, you will pass the end of a red brick building on your left, where you will enter into a courtyard. Keep your dog on a lead in the courtyard. Turn left and pass Barn Rooms on your left. Pass the old stables and toilets, also on your left. At the end of the courtyard, pass through an arched gateway. Continue straight ahead, where you will cross a cobbled path, and go through a gap in the holly hedge. Continue on a path beside the trees. On reaching the end of the path, go through the gate on your left. You will reach an access road. Deer and livestock may be in the area from this point, so keep your dog under close control, or on a lead.

Turn right and pass the mansion on your right. Continue on a wide worn path, beside the metal fence on your right. Mature parkland trees are scattered amongst the grassland.

Continue beside the metal fence on your right, and follow the right hand bend. Descend gradually and

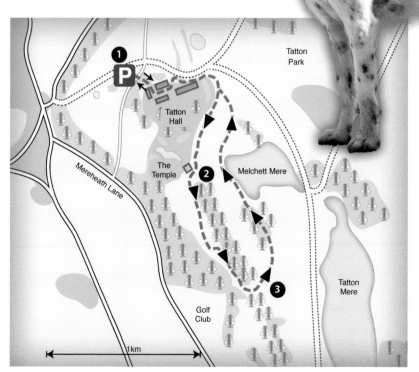

as you reach fairly level ground the path veers away from the fence. Continue on the wide grass path with the metal fence now over on your right. On reaching a stock fence pass through the gate. You will have a large pond/lake on your far left. Continue straight ahead, and you will reach and continue beside a low concrete wall. This is known as a tank bridge and was built during the Second World War. The ministry of defence used the estate as a training ground. Before reaching the end of the tank bridge veer to your right.

❷ You will pass a monument within the fenced garden on your right. At the end of the metal fence turn right, and continue on the worn path, with a post and rail fence over on your left. Veer to your left, where you will reach the corner of the post and rail fence. Turn left and continue on the worn grass path beside the post and rail fence on your left. Beyond the fence is the original avenue of trees, which was planted to provide a grand entrance to the mansion.

When the grass path forks, take the path on your right, which crosses over open grassland. You will pass a fence corner on your right. Mature Scot's pine trees are on your left. As you continue you will pass a tree inclosure on your right. As you pass the inclosure you will have trees on your right and a red brick wall beyond. A little further along, the path will merge with your original path, beside the post and rail fence. At the end of the post and rail fence turn left. Continue between post and rail fence. At the end of the fence you will reach another tank bridge on your right.

❸ Cross the wide grass path, with the tank bridge on your right. Continue straight ahead and descend on the narrow path between grass hillocks. On reaching another path with a mature oak tree straight ahead, turn left. You will soon reach another wider grass path. Turn left and then almost immediately take the path on your right. Soon after cross another path and continue straight ahead. Just after, on reaching another path turn left and head for the trees.

Continue amongst the mature trees, but keep over to your right, close to the edge of the trees, as the path isn't obvious. The lake is over on your right. As you leave the trees, you will descend close to the water's edge. Continue on the worn grass path. Take a path which veers to your left. On reaching another path turn right. You will soon reach close to the water's edge once more, amongst the tussock grass and juncus. As you pass the lake the grass path widens. Head for the fence and pass through the gate.

Continue straight ahead, where you will have views of the mansion. Ignore paths on your left and right and continue straight ahead. As you continue take the path on your left, and you will soon reach a familiar spot, with the metal fence on your left. Continue on the familiar path, and when you pass the mansion you can either go through the gate on your left and retrace your steps back to the courtyard and facilities, or continue beside the entrance road where you will reach back to the car park.

3. Quarry Bank

Easy - 1.7 miles - 1hrs

The National Trust owns Quarry Bank. It is now a museum and country park, but was once a working cotton mill. The circular walk will pass the mill and then after crossing through farmland you will enter into wonderful broadleaved woodland. You will reach and continue beside the River Bollin, where your dog can have a cool down at the oxbow, where there is a beach area. There may be cattle on a small section of the walk. There are no roads.

How to get there – Take junction 5 off the M56 and follow the brown signs for Quarry Bank

Grid Reference – SJ 834830

Postcode – SK9 4LA

Parking – Pay on entrance to car park

Facilities – There are toilets and a café

You will need – Dog lead, dog bags

The Walk

❶ Keep your dog on a lead to begin with. From the car park, make your way to the information centre, which is signed for Entrance. Take the path between the information centre and the welcome board. Descend on the sealed path beside the split rail fence. On reaching another path turn left (continue straight ahead). Descend the steps on your right. Turn right on reaching the wide path (facilities are on your left).

Ascend gently and keep your dog on a lead or under close control, as there is access for vehicles. Ignore a footpath on your left, signed for Morley. Ascend a little steeper between the sandstone walls. Ignore another footpath on your left, which cuts back on itself. Soon after on reaching a fingerpost turn left, following the sign for Styal Village. Continue on the path, with a split rail fence on your left and a field beyond, and a timber fence on your right. Keep your dog under close control or on a lead. Pass through a gate and continue straight ahead through the middle of a field.

At the end of the field pass through a gate, cross a track and go through the gate opposite. Continue straight

ahead on the edge of a field. You will pass a pond beyond the split rail fence on your left. At the end of the field, pass through a gate and turn left. Soon after, turn left again, before you reach Northcliffe Chapel.

❷ Continue on a path with a hedgerow on your right and a split rail fence and field on your left.

At the end of the path pass through a gate, cross a track and continue straight ahead into woodland. Just after, when you reach a gully, take the path ahead and to your right. Continue through the mixed broadleaved wood, with the gully on your left. You will pass a metal footbridge on your left. Continue straight ahead. As the path veers to your left, there is a steep slope on your right. Descend the steps and turn right half way down. Keep your dog under close control, as there is a bridge ahead with a drop, if your dog jumps onto the wall. Continue to descend the steps, and then turn left.

You will reach and cross the lovely stone bridge 'Chapel Bridge'. Ascend some steps and then turn left. There is a deep ravine on your left. Just after, turn right and ascend on the path. There is a deep ravine now on your right. The path has a switch back. Continue on the woodland edge with the ravine again on your left. Pass amongst rhododendrons on both sides of the path. Continue to descend with some steps in places.

You will reach another wide path, and an oxbow in the river below on your right. Continue straight ahead on the wide path. There is a path on your right, where you can detour to allow your dog access to the beach area of the river, providing the flow is steady. Continue straight ahead on the path, which continues beside the river. You will pass another section of river with an ox bow and a bridge on your right.

Continue straight ahead, and soon after the path bends sharply to your left. On reaching another path, turn right (straight ahead as you merge onto it). Continue beside the river. You will reach Kingfisher Bridge. Cross this and ascend with some steps. Beech trees dominate the wood here. You leave the river behind, and there is a ravine on your left.

❸ You will reach a path on your right, next to a sign on your left (just before a metal footbridge ahead and to your left). Take this path. There is a stock fence on your right, and a Tudor house on your far right, and a hedgerow on your left with a field beyond. On reaching a gate pass through it and cross a track. Go through a gate opposite and continue between the hedgerow and stock fence. At the end of the path put your dog on a lead, and pass through another gate.

On reaching the tarmac track turn right. You are now in a familiar spot. Descend between the sandstone walls, where you will reach back to the steps on your left for the car park.

4. Southern Woods

Easy - 1.5 miles - 1hr 30min

This is a pleasant circular walk, within the grounds of the National Trust estate. The walk is predominantly in woodlands, some of which are woodland carr (wet woods) and you will walk beside the River Bollin in places, before returning across meadows and on the edge of farmland. There may be cattle on this walk, which are used for conservation grazing, but they are well used to dog walkers. There are no roads.

How to get there – Take junction 5 off the M56 and follow the brown signs for Quarry Bank

Grid Reference – SJ 834830

Postcode – SK9 4LA

Parking – Pay on entrance to the car park

Facilities – There are toilets and a café

You will need – Dog lead, dog bags

The Walk

❶ Keep your dog on a lead to begin with. From the car park, make your way to the information centre which is signed for Entrance (depending on where you have parked your car). Take the path between the information centre and the welcome board. Descend on the sealed path beside the split rail fence. You will reach another path and continue straight ahead. Descend the steps on your right. At the bottom of the steps turn left on the wide path.

Pass the information office and shop on your left, and continue straight ahead. Pass through a gate (not the one to enter into the gardens), where you will pass a sluice gate below on your right. Pass a play area on your right, and continue on the path between hedgerows.

❷ You will see a weir on your far right. Take the path on your right, cross a footbridge and continue beside a millpond on your left. As you continue, you will have a river on your right. You will reach the main path once again. Turn right, and continue on the path on the edge of the wood. The path will narrow a little

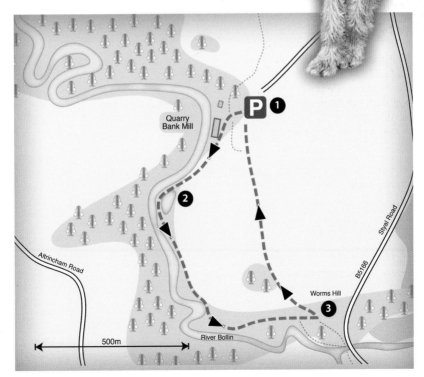

and you will ascend gently. The river is below on your right. On your left you will pass exposed sandstone, which has been quarried in the past.

The path is wider again here. A little further on you will reach and continue beside the chestnut paling on your left. As you reach a post and rail fence on your right there is an oxbow in the river. Cross Heron's Pool footbridge. Continue on the path between stock fence and chestnut paling. Descend on the path, with alder carr woodland on your right.

Continue on the path and as you see a gate in the distance veer to your right. Continue on a slightly raised path through the willow-dominated wet woodland. You will see the river again on your right. Call your dogs close when you reach a short section of post and rail fence and a white stone post on your right, as there is a road ahead. At the end of the path, pass through a kissing gate and turn left.

❸ The road is parallel for a short section here. Ascend gently on a sealed path. Just after, go through the kissing gate on your left. There may be livestock, so keep your dog under close control or on a lead.

Here you will leave the road behind. Cross the hilly field on the well-worn path. Ignore a path which veers to your left, and continue straight ahead. Ascend to a gate. Pass through the gate and continue to ascend on an old cobble path. At the end of the cobble path continue between hedgerows, with fields beyond. The hedge on your right ends, and is replaced by a stock fence.

At the end of the path, you will reach and pass through a farm gate. There may be livestock, so keep your dog under close control or on a lead, and continue on the field edge with a hedgerow on your left. At the end of the field go through the gate, cross a path and continue straight ahead, where you will reach the car park on your right.

Countryside Dog Walks - Cheshire

5. Lindow Common

Medium - 3.4 miles - 2hrs

This circular walk passes through Lindow Common, where you will see heathland, grassland and copses of trees. There is a large fenced pond within the common. You will then enter into Newgate Nature Reserve, which was once a landfill site, but is now young woodland with grassland. There is a slight ascent, which takes you through the young woodland. You will then continue between hedgerows, as you pass beside farmland. There is a short section where you cross a field, so you may encounter livestock. There are quiet access tracks and a short section of lane.

How to get there – Lindow Common is located in Wilmslow. From the M56 turn off at junction 6. Follow the sign for Wilmslow on the A538. Continue through the tunnel on the A538. Continue further along the road and just as you enter the outskirts of the town look for a pub; The Boddington Arms and a Premier Inn on your right hand side, turn right immediately after, on Racecourse Road. The car park for the common is just after on your left.

Grid Reference – SJ 833813   **Postcode** – SK9 5LR

Parking – Free in the car park

Facilities – There are no facilities

You will need – Dog lead, poop bags and water for your dog in hot weather

The Walk

❶ From the car park enter the common from the main entrance; continue on the surfaced path through the middle of grassland/heath. The path has a series of bends. Pass between mature silver birch and oak trees and then you will reach another path and a small fenced lake, known locally as Black Lake.

Turn left and continue on the surfaced path, with the lake on your right. Ignore any narrow paths. At the furthest end of the lake you will merge with another path from your left. Continue beside the lake but shortly afterward leave the sealed path and take a path on your left.

❷ Continue on the wide path, and soon after, cross a narrow path. Continue on the path straight ahead, which will veer to your right.

You will pass an area of gorse on your right. The path widens again and there is heather on both sides of the path. There is a stock fence over on your left. You will reach another path at the corner of the stock fence. Turn left and continue beside the stock fence on your left. Put your dog on a lead, as there is a road ahead.

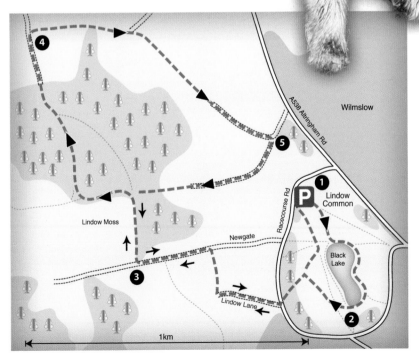

At the end of the path, pass through a kissing gate. Cross the road and continue on Lindow Lane. Ignore a bridleway on your left and continue, passing a number of houses. At the end of the lane, you will reach Racecourse Farm. Turn right and continue on the bridleway. Keep your dog under close control, as there is a lane ahead. Continue between the hedgerows and at the end of the path put your dog on a lead and turn left onto the lane.

Continue on the lane and shortly before a 'no through road' sign turn right and enter into Newgate Nature Reserve.

❸ Pass through a metal kissing gate and continue on a narrow grass path beside a post and rail fence on your left and woods on your right. The bridleway continues on your left, on the track. On reaching the end of the fence, you will merge with the bridleway.

Shortly after, ignore a footpath which descends on your right. Just after, before a slight hill, turn left on the bridleway. Continue between the trees on a surfaced path. You will reach a path with steps on your right. Take this path and continue through the young oak/ash woodland. Continue straight ahead, where you will merge once again with a bridleway. Ignore a bridleway on your right and continue straight ahead, where you will soon descend.

On reaching level ground pass beside a horse stile. Continue beside a ditch on your right. You will leave the wood and continue on the bridleway between fenced fields. Put your dog on a lead and pass through a gate. Continue between the hedgerows. Pass farm buildings and then a house on your right. Turn right immediately after the house and continue between hedgerows.

❹ Continue on the grass path between ditches and hedgerows, with fields beyond. When the path widens and veers to your left, take the footpath on your right, put your dog on a lead, or under close control and pass through the gate. Continue straight ahead on the edge of the field with a ditch and barbed fence on your right.

On reaching the end of the field, pass through a kissing gate and continue between the hedgerows, with fields beyond. Keep your dog under close control or on a lead, as there are free-range hens and an access track ahead. Pass a house on your right and continue on an access track.

❺ At the end of the field on your right, turn right and continue on another track. There are fields on your right. As you continue you will pass a house on your left and pass beside a vehicle barrier. Continue on the track between fields with mature trees and hedgerows. Pass allotments on your right. You will pass agricultural buildings on your left. At the end of the track ascend the steps and turn left. You are now in a familiar spot. Retrace your steps on the path, beside the post and rail fence. At the end of the path, go through the metal kissing gate, put your dog on a lead and continue straight ahead.

Turn left on reaching the lane. Immediately after you pass the house on your right, there is a bridleway on your right, which you should ignore. Continue on the lane and take the familiar bridleway on your right, a little further along. At the end of the path, put your dog on a lead and pass through the gate. Turn left on the byway. At the end of the byway, cross a road and pass through the gate on the opposite side.

On reaching the end of the stock fences, continue straight ahead on the wide path and cross the common. On reaching another path turn left. After a short distance cross anther narrow path and continue straight ahead. On reaching another path, turn right. You will soon reach a surfaced path. Turn left and continue to the car park.

6. Ladybrook Valley

Easy - 2 miles - 1hr

This is a fairly level circular walk, starting on the Middlewood Way, which is a disused railway. This is a popular route in the area for dog walkers, cyclists and horse riding. There is a path which is separate from the bridleway. You will cross a couple of horse paddocks before reaching the Macclesfield Canal. There is a short section on a quiet lane.

How to get there – Junction 6 off the M56. Follow the sign for A538 Hale/ Wilmslow/Macclesfield. Follow signs for A34 Manchester/ Airport/ Handforth. Turn off the A34 following the sign for Bramhall and Poynton. Continue to follow the sign for Poynton (A5149). On reaching the church in the centre of Poynton, take the second turning on the roundabout onto Park Lane. Continue on the road, which then becomes Coppice Lane. Look for a left turn on to Shrigley Road North (if you go over a bridge you have just passed it). Turn right onto Lyme Road, where you will reach the car park on your left.

Grid Reference – SJ 945833   **Postcode** – SK12 1TH

Parking – Nelson Pit car park

Facilities – There are toilets in the car park

You will need – Dog lead, dog bags

The Walk

❶ From the car park, go back to the entrance and cross the road. Continue straight ahead and descend the steps to enter on the Middlewood Way, which is a disused railway. Turn right and pass under the road bridge. Continue on the surfaced path. The path is also a cycle path and a bridleway.

A little further on you can chose to leave the main path, which allows some distance from horse riders. Veer right and ascend on the narrow path between hedgerows. There is a pony paddock beyond the hedge on your right. You will descend to pass under a bridge. Ascend again if you wish to avoid passing close to horse riders.

Descend again to pass under bridge 17, and continue on the main path. There is a ditch on both sides of the path. A little further on you have the option of ascending the steps on your right to continue on the path, away from the bridleway. Descend the steps, where you will reach bridge 18.

❷ Before going under the bridge turn right. Put your dog on a lead and ascend the steps, where you will reach a road.

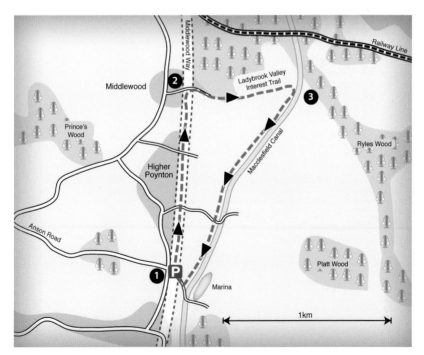

Turn right on the road. Cross the head of a driveway for Pool House Farm. Continue straight ahead on a grass verge, and then go through a gap in the fence beside a fingerpost. Continue between fences, and just after, ignore a kissing gate on your left. On reaching a gate, put your dog on a lead and pass through it. Continue straight ahead, where just after you will reach a farm track. Continue straight ahead, and pass farm buildings on your right.

Go between a hedgerow and a pony paddock, where you will reach a kissing gate. Keep your dog under close control or on a lead, as there may be horses in the field. Pass through the kissing gate and continue on the edge of the field beside the electric fence on your left. At the end of the field, go through another kissing gate. Continue on the edge of another field, with a hedgerow on your left.

At the end of the field, pass through the small gate. Turn right on a quiet lane, keeping your dog under close control or on a lead. Ascend gently to the end of the lane. Cross another lane and continue straight ahead, where you will join the canal towpath.

❸ Turn right and pass under bridge 13. There are boat moorings on the opposite side of the canal. Continue beside the canal on your left, with a hedgerow on your right, and fields beyond.

Pass a fingerpost and stile on your right and continue beside the canal. There are silver birch trees on your right. Pass under bridge 14 and continue on the towpath, which is now sealed. There are moorings for boats now on both sides of the canal. You will reach the car park beside the canal as you continue. Pass through the kissing gate on your right, where you enter back into the car park.

7. Lyme Park

Medium - 1.9 miles - 1hr 30min

This is a wonderful walk in the grounds of the beautiful Georgian estate, now owned by the National Trust. You will pass through woodland and then ascend gently across sloping pasture. You will have the most amazing views after a gradual ascent, looking over the beautiful rolling countryside for miles. At your highest point you will reach the hunting lodge, which is a beautiful tower, built in 1737. There may be sheep and deer in places throughout the walk. There is a stream for your dog to cool off and get a drink.

How to get there – From Stockport, take the A6, signed for Buxton. Lyme Park will be signed off the main road, just as you leave High Lane.

Grid Reference – SJ 965825

Postcode – SK12 2NR

Parking – Admission charge; see National Trust website for details

Facilities – There are toilets and a café

You will need – Dog leads, dog bags

The Walk

❶ Keep your dog on a lead to begin with. From the car park head towards the visitor centre. With your back to the visitor centre entrance, walk towards the pond in front of you. Continue on the tarmac drive, with the pond over on your left. You will pass a disabled parking bay on your right. Take a surfaced path on your left and continue beside the pond, with the toilet block on your right.

Cross a footbridge and then turn right. Continue on this path, where you will pass through a children's play area. Keep your dog on a lead, until you have passed the play equipment. On reaching a right hand bend, ignore a path on your left and continue straight ahead. Ignore another path on your left. Your dog can get access to a stream on your right just after.

You will see a large gate ahead. Veer to your left before reaching the gate. Pass through a small gate. Turn left on a worn grass path, and keep your dog under close control or on a lead, as there is an access road ahead and deer/livestock may be

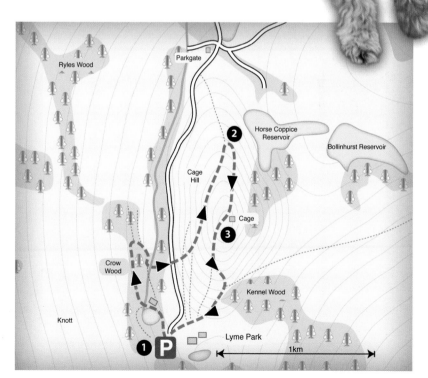

grazing in the area. Ascend a hill, where you will meet a wider grass path. Turn left on this path. Cross the access road and continue straight ahead ascending on the wide grass path.

On reaching another grass path you will see the hall on your right. Cross this path and continue straight ahead, but veer to your left. As you ascend you will see a building ahead. This was used as a hunting lodge, and was known as 'The Cage'. You will reach another grass path. Turn left on this path, and continue on a fairly level path, which cuts across the gently sloping hillside. On a clear day you will have views, to which will increase as you continue.

❷ As you begin to descend you will reach a stony path. Here another path will merge with the path you are on from your right and behind. Take this wide grass path and ascend to the hunting lodge. You will have new views now on your left. Pass the lodge, where you will see two paths. If you are standing with your back to the centre of the lodge and sundial, take the path which is ahead but to your left, not the path straight ahead.

❸ Descend on the wide grass path, ignoring any narrow paths on your left and right. The path may get a little boggy as you reach the bottom of the hill. Ascend for a short distance and you will meet a tarmac path. Keep your dog under close control, as there may be vehicles on this track. Turn right and descend gently beside estate fencing on your left. You will pass two access roads on your left in close succession. Shortly after you will pass another access road on your left. The hall is over on your left.

Continue toward the gateway for the circular drive of the hall. Just as you reach the gateway take the path on your right, with steps. This path will lead you back to the car park and visitor centre.

8. Marbury Park

Easy - 3.75 miles - 2hrs

This is a delightful circular walk through wonderful woodlands, beside the beautiful Budworth Mere, and across quiet farmland, where after a short section of road you will reach the Trent and Mersey Canal. You can enjoy a peaceful walk along the towpath before returning back through Marbury Park, where you will reach an impressive lime avenue, which once led to a grand hall. Your dog will enjoy running through the woods and into the mere. There may be livestock in parts of the walk, and there is a short section of road.

How to get there – From Northwich, follow the signs to Anderton Boat Lift and Marbury Country Park. Continue passed the boat lift and follow signs for Marbury Park.

Grid Reference – SJ 650765

Postcode – CW9 6AT

Parking – Pay and display

Facilities – There are toilets and a covered sitting area

You will need – Dog lead, dog bags

The Walk

❶ Facing the ticket machine, go to your left and continue on the edge of the car park. Leave the car park, pass a meadow on your right and go through a gate, then turn left. Take the path on the left of the toilet block. Pass between trees and lawn areas. Ignore a path on your left.

The path becomes tarmac; on meeting another path, turn right. The path will bend to the right and you will see Budworth Mere on your left through the trees. Turn left to descend the wide, sandstone steps. On reaching the bird hide, turn right to follow the water's edge, with mixed broadleaved trees on your right.

You may either take the steps on the left, which pass the boathouse, or stay on the wider path under the trees; both paths join ahead. Continue alongside the mere until the path veers away to the right. You will reach a fenced pond 'The Ice Pond'. Take the narrow path on your left as you reach the gate to enter the viewing platform for the pond. If you reach the fingerpost you have missed the path.

Continue back towards the lake and turn right on another path. You will have a ditch and then the lake on your left. You will reach and cross an arched bridge on your left. Continue on the

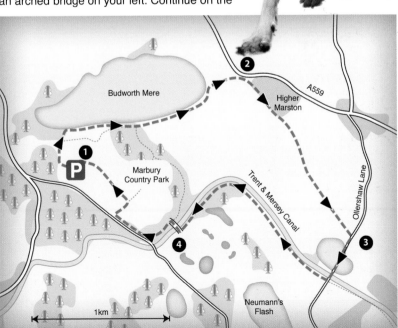

worn path, which ascends a bank and then continue beside the mere. There is a stock fence and field on your right. As you continue beside the mere, you will reach a kissing gate. Put your dog on a lead, or under close control and pass through the kissing gate. There may be livestock and there is a busy road ahead. Continue on the edge of a field with a stock fence on your left.

❷ You will reach another kissing gate in the corner of the field. Don't go through the kissing gate but turn right. Continue on the edge of the field, beside a hedgerow on your left. Ascend gently and you will soon pass houses on your left beyond the hedge. At the end of the field pass through another kissing gate and continue on the edge of another field. At the end of the field pass through a kissing gate and cross a track. Go through the kissing gate on the opposite side. Keep your dog under close control or on a lead and continue on the edge of the field, with a stock fence on your right.

Pass through anther kissing gate and then cross through the middle of the field. Go through another kissing gate and turn left. Continue on the edge of another field with a hedgerow on your left. At the end of the field pass through a kissing gate. Continue on the edge of the field, with a stock fence on your right. You will see another mere on your far right.

Pass a farmyard on your right, put your dog on a lead and then go through the kissing gate. Continue on the access track and turn right on reaching the road.

❸ Pass the mere on your right. After about 150 yards cross a canal bridge and then turn right. On reaching the canal towpath turn left. Continue beside the canal until you reach a canal bridge. Take the exit on your left to access and cross the bridge.

❹ Turn left, where you will now find yourself back in the woodlands of Marbury Park. Follow alongside the canal on your left to begin with, and then the path will bend sharply to your right, leaving the canal. Ignore a path on your left and continue straight ahead. You will come near to farmland on your right. Stay on the wider, woodland path.

On reaching another path, turn right, walking between farmland, with a hedgerow on your right and stock fence on your left. Go through the kissing gate on your left and follow the path through the middle of the field (there may be cattle grazing). Pass through the kissing gate on the other side, into silver birch woodland.

You will pass a lovely flower meadow on your left. On meeting another path, cross this to go straight ahead. There is an impressive lime avenue on your right. You can walk between the lime avenue or stay on the path. Take the next path on the left, passing the interpretation panel and returning to the car park.

9. Neumann's Flash
Med. - 2.7 miles - 1hr 30min

This circular walk is very pleasant, and the paths are fairly level and well surfaced. You will begin on the path which continues around both flashes, but they are fenced and screened off with trees and scrub. You will leave the flash and continue through meadows, where your dog can run around in the open space. There are pockets of woodland and scrub amongst the meadows. You will see an old pipeline for parts of your walk, which remains from the old salt and ash works. There are no roads except for a short section on an access road, and there are no livestock.

How to get there –From the centre of Northwich, follow the sign for Manchester on the A559 and the brown sign for Lion Saltworks. On reaching the roundabout, take the second exit, following the sign for Warrington on the B5075, and the brown sign for Lion Saltworks. You will see the layby on your left, shortly after leaving the town centre.

Grid Reference – SJ 669752   **Postcode** – CW9 6ES

Parking – Layby on the B5075

Facilities – There are no facilities

You will need – Dog lead, dog bags and water for your dog

The Walk

❶ From the layby, face the road and turn left, and continue on the pavement. Near to the end of the layby, go between the fences on your left. Continue on the worn grass path. Pass through the kissing gate on your left. Continue straight ahead, and just afterwards, on reaching a fingerpost turn right, following the sign for Neumann's Flash.

Continue between post and rail fences on the gravel path, which is also a bridleway, so you may encounter horses. You will glimpse the flash on your left in places, where the trees allow. Ignore a path on your right, which crosses a bridge. A little further on pass a path on your left which leads to a bird hide. Ignore a path on your right and continue straight ahead, following the sign for Witton Mill and Marbury Lane.

❷ On reaching a metal gate and a finger post turn right, and follow the sign for Dairy House Meadows. Cross the bridge and ascend on a sealed path between fences. Continue round a sharp bend and descend. Ascend again and continue through a meadow on a surfaced path. On reaching a fingerpost turn right, following the sign for Marbury Country

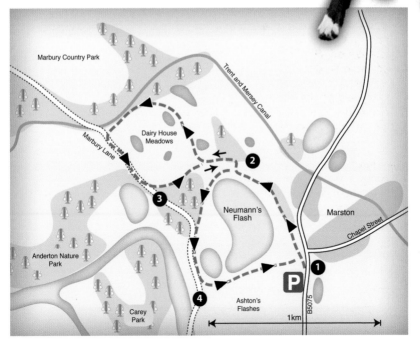

Park. Pass through a kissing gate and continue on the path between a hedge and a post and rail fence.

There is a pond on your right beyond the fence, and fields on your left. Shortly after, you will pass a pond on your left. As you continue you will have trees on both sides of the path. You will reach a canal beyond a hedge on your right. Pass an entrance onto the canal and then a bridge, which goes over the canal. Continue on the path beside the post and rail fence on your left.

Ignore a path on your right, and continue round a left bend. On reaching a kissing gate on your right, put your dog on a lead or under close control. Pass through the kissing gate and turn left on the access road, and follow the sign for Ashton's and Neumann's Flash on the fingerpost.

❸ On reaching another fingerpost turn left, and follow the sign for Dairy House Meadows / Neumann's Flash. Pass beside the gate, over a horse stile. Continue on the surfaced path, beside the post and rail fence on your left, with trees beyond. You will soon reach a familiar spot, on reaching another fingerpost. Continue straight ahead, and retrace your steps back to the flash. Just before you reach the flash, you will have views across Neumann's flash, after an accent. On reaching the path beside the flash turn right.

Pass through a gap beside a metal gate and continue straight ahead, ascending gently between the fences. There are views across the flash on your left. You will pass a path on your left, which leads to another bird hide. Shortly afterwards you will pass a path on your right, which leads to Marbury Lane and Anderton Nature Reserve. Now there is some distance between the path and the flash.

You will reach a wide area, with a kissing gate on your right and a metal gate and kissing gate straight ahead. Don't go through the gate, but turn left.

❹ Ascend gently on the surfaced path between silver birch trees. Neumann's Flash is on your left, and Ashton's Flash is on your right. Pass a path which leads to a hide on your left. On reaching a gate, pass through the kissing gate, where you will reach a familiar spot. Put your dog on a lead and continue straight ahead, where you will pass through another kissing gate to reach the road.

10. Anderton Nature Reserve Med. - 3.2 miles 2hr

Anderton Nature Reserve is found on the edge of Northwich Town Centre. The site was once a salt and soda ash mine. Today it is predominantly meadows, ponds and pockets of woodland. You will see the old pipeline beside some of the paths, which remain from its past industry. The walk follows beside the Witton Brook and the River Weaver. You will also pass briefly beside the Trent and Mersey Canal. There is lots of open space where your dog can run through the meadows. There are no roads and no livestock.

How to get there –From the centre of Northwich, follow the sign for Manchester on the A559 and the brown sign for Lion Saltworks. On reaching the roundabout, take the first exit onto Leicester Street, which is signed Waste Disposal Site. Turn next right, following the sign for Waste Disposal. Continue on the road, where you will go under a height barrier before reaching the car park on your left.

Grid Reference – SJ 663748   **Postcode** – CW9 6DA

Parking – Free in Witton Mill car park

Facilities – There are no facilities

You will need – Dog lead, poop bags

The Walk

1 From the car park, have your back to the entrance and turn right. Go to the furthest end, and take the surfaced path on the left hand side of a gate. There is a reed bed on your left, with a brook beyond, and a wire fence with trees beyond it on your right. Shortly after, pass through a kissing gate and continue straight ahead. There is a field beyond the fence now, on your right.

Continue on the path, where you will reach another kissing gate. Pass through the kissing gate and ascend gently, meandering through the mixed broadleaved wood.

2 On reaching a tarmac path, turn left and cross a bridge. Ascend gently, and shortly after, turn left. Follow the sign on the finger post for Anderton boat lift.

Shortly after, on meeting another path, turn left, again following the sign for Anderton boat lift. There are reeds on your left, with a river beyond and there is a bank on your right. Pass a set of steps on your right, and continue straight ahead on the surfaced path. You will reach and continue beside a post and rail fence on your right.

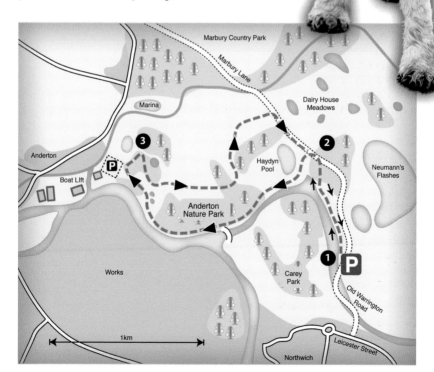

Cross a bridge and take the narrow path straight ahead. There is a short fence on your left, with the river beyond and a bank with scrub on your right. As you continue another path joins from your right and you will pass a bridge on your left. Continue straight ahead, descend the steps and continue on the surfaced path.

You will see the salt works on your left and ahead, beyond the river. As you reach close to the salt works, on the opposite side of the river, the trees clear on your left and you will cross a footbridge. Continue beside the river and soon you will cross another footbridge. Just after, on reaching another path turn left. Continue beside the river, with a meadow on your right.

Continue on the track round a right hand bend. Ascend on the sealed track. At the top of the hill, ignore a path on your right. Put your dog on a lead and continue straight ahead, where you will reach a car park. Turn right and stay on the outer edge of the car park. When you reach a path in the corner of the car park turn right.

❸ Follow the sealed path veering left and then right. You pass a pond on your left with woodland on your right as you veer right. On meeting another path turn left then turn immediately right. You are now on a wide track.

Continue beside a hedgerow on your left, with a fishing pond beyond it. Pass beside a vehicle barrier and ascend gently. Continue on the surfaced path. On reaching a fork, take the path on your left following the sign on the fingerpost for Uplands Woodland / Dairy House Meadow / Marbury Park. This is a large meadow surrounded by trees. Follow the path with the meadow on your right.

Ignore a path on your right, which is signposted for Carden's Ferry Bridge and continue straight ahead. The path veers to the left as you leave the meadow. Cross a bridge over the river, and then ascend a little. You will pass a meadow on your right. Ascend a little once more and then the area opens up with lovely meadows on your left.

Ignore a path on your right and a little further ahead you will reach an access road. Turn right on the quiet road, keeping your dog under close control. There is a stream below the bank on your right. Ignore a path on your left and continue on the access road. You will reach a familiar spot. Ignore the path on your right and cross the bridge. Turn right just after, and then retrace your steps on the path through the wood. Continue beside the river, where you will eventually arrive back at the car park.

11. Tegg's Nose

Chall. - 1.7 miles - 1hr 30min

This walk begins with a steep ascent through broadleaved woods. You will climb out of the wood on an open grass hill to reach the edge of Tegg's Nose, where you will gain wonderful views. You will continue on good surfaced paths, where you will pass an old quarry, with remnants of quarry equipment on display. Continue amongst the heather and after crossing on the edge of two fields you will return on a familiar path. There may be livestock for parts of this walk, but there are no roads.

How to get there – From Macclesfield town centre close to the junction for the A536 (Congleton Road), take the A523 heading for Leek. Soon after, turn left when you see the sign for Langley and Wincle. Follow the sign for Langley and Macclesfield Forest. Continue on the road through the village of Langley and turn left onto Holehouse Lane. At the end of the lane, turn left and continue between the stone walls to the car park.

Grid Reference – SJ 944717

Postcode – SK11 0NB

Parking – Free in the car park

Facilities – There are no facilities

You will need – Dog lead, dog bags and water for your dog

The Walk

❶ From the car park with your back to the entrance, take the path on your left, signed Grit Stone Trail. Ascend the steps on the steeply wooded hillside. Pass through a kissing gate and continue beside a stone wall on your left. The gradient lessens a little as you continue. You will reach another kissing gate. Put your dog on a lead or under close control, as there may be livestock. Pass through the kissing gate and continue to ascend gradually. You will rise above the treetops. The path veers away from the wall, and you will continue to ascend through open heathland/grassland, following the waymarker.

Ascend the stone slab steps and then pass through a gate. Turn right on a surfaced path, with wire fence on your right. There is a heather covered hillside on your left. On a clear day there are wonderful views ahead and on your right. Ignore the footpath on your right and pass a lovely crafted stone memorial bench on your left. Just after this, there is a path on your right which leads to a viewing area and bench. Continue on the main path and ascend for a short distance.

48

As the path bends sharply to your left, continue straight ahead. Pass a quarry face on your left, and shortly after you will reach old disused quarry equipment.

2 There are interpretation panels, which show the history of the area. Continue on the path, where you will descend gradually. On reaching a fork, take the path ahead but slightly to your right. Descend the steps and then turn left.

3 Ignore a path on your left shortly after, and pass through the small gate. Keep your dog under close control if there are cattle grazing.

Continue straight ahead beside a stone wall on your right on the edge of the field. Descend to the corner of the field and go through the gateway. Cross the edge of another field beside the stone wall. Pass through a kissing gate and turn left on a tarmac track. Ascend gently between a bank and a hedgerow. On reaching a kissing gate, pass through it and continue on the track. There are views on your right. At the end of the tarmac track go through the gate on your right.

Continue on a grass path, beside a wire fence on your right. Shortly after, go through a gate on your right. You are now in a familiar spot. Retrace your steps and descend to the car park.

12. Macclesfield Forest
Chall. - 3.3 miles - 2hr

Macclesfield Forest is on the edge of Macclesfield town. The forest is predominantly a plantation of coniferous trees, but there are mixed broadleaved trees on the edge of the plantation. All the paths are surfaced, and after a steady ascent, with a steeper section toward the end, you will reach lovely views into the valley where you will see three reservoirs. There's a pond where your dog can cool off in hot weather. There are no livestock, and only a short section of road.

How to get there – From Macclesfield town centre, close to the junction for the A536 (Congleton Road), take the A523 heading for Leek. Soon after, turn left when you see the sign for Langley and Wincle. Follow the sign for Langley and Macclesfield Forest. Continue on the road through the village of Langley and turn right on reaching the Leather Smithy pub. You will reach several parking bays on your left.

Grid Reference – SJ953715   **Postcode** – SK11 0NE

Parking – In the lay-by beside Ridgegate Reservoir.

Facilities – There are toilets close to the start of your walk.

You will need – Dog leads, poop bags

The Walk

❶ Put your dog on a lead to begin this walk. With the reservoir on your right, walk along the road. Depending on where along the road you have parked there may be a footpath on your left beside the road. On reaching the end of the reservoir take the footpath on your right. The footpath continues along the road, therefore keep your dog on a lead or under close control. You will pass a gap in the stone wall onto the road. Continue on the path with the forest on your right.

On reaching a metal motorbike barrier/entrance to the road, cross the head of a road, and continue on the path on the opposite side. Keep your dog under close control, as there is a road on your left, beyond the stone wall and you will soon reach a car park ahead.

❷ Cross the edge of the car park, and then pass a visitor centre and toilets on your right. Pass an interpretation panel, which is covered. Continue on the surfaced path, where you will pass between another motorbike barrier.

Take the path which veers to your right. Ascend gently, where you leave the road behind. The path soon has a sharp right hand bend. Continue beside the stock fence on your right. The fence veers off away from your path, and you will continue

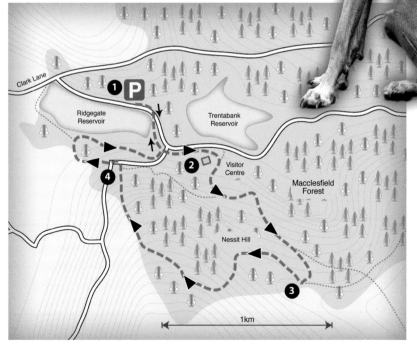

to ascend. You will pass a path on your right and a fingerpost. Continue straight ahead, following the sign for Shuttingsloe. Ascend more steeply, and you will reach a post and rail fence, a fingerpost and a track.

Turn left on the forest track, and continue following the sign for Shuttingsloe. Shortly after on reaching another fingerpost turn right, again following the sign for Shuttingsloe. Ascend on the path, with a stone wall on your right. Veer away from the wall just before the path levels out a little. Continue on the elevated path, which cuts through the wooded hillside.

❸ After another ascent, you will reach a gate. Continue through the motorcycle barrier beside the gate, and take the immediate right turn, following the sign on the fingerpost for Forest Bridleway. Ascend on the path, which has a series of bends. The path gets a little steeper as you continue, where you will gain views on your right and behind you.

The path levels out, and a little further along you will reach and continue beside a dilapidated stone wall on your right. At the end of the stone wall there is a viewing area on your right, where you can see three reservoirs and the hills beyond. This is the highest point of the walk. You will begin to descend now through the forest. Ignore a cycle track on your right just after you begin your descent.

You will continue around a sharp left bend, and pass a post and rail fence on your right. As you continue on the track, you will pass a pond on your left. A little further along you will continue on the edge of the forest, with a stone wall and a field on your left. There are views to a reservoir in the distance. At the end of the field you will continue through the forest. Continue on the path, and when you see a vehicle barrier ahead, call your dog close, as there is a quiet road beyond the barrier. On reaching the barrier put your dog on a lead, and go through the gate and turn left on the road.

❹ On reaching a sharp bend in the road, leave the road and continue straight ahead. Pass between the motorcycle barrier and continue on the surfaced path. The path narrows and winds through the wood. You will descend and reach the edge of Ridgegate reservoir.

Turn right on the path, and continue beside the deer fence on your left, with the reservoir beyond it. The path undulates through the forest, and veers away from the reservoir.

As you near a stone wall, keep your dog under close control, as there is an entrance onto a quiet road. There is a stream on your left as you reach the wall, where your dog can get a drink. Continue beside the stone wall on your right, but keep your dog under close control or on a lead. Soon after you will reach another motorcycle barrier on your right, and a familiar spot. Continue past the barrier, and retrace your steps beside the stone wall, with the road beyond. At the end of the path, continue on the road, where you will reach back to your car.

13. Delamere *(Old Pale)* Medium - 3.6 miles - 2hr

This forest walk is ideal for dogs, having very little road and no livestock. It has some streams, where your dog can get a drink. There are some broadleaved trees amongst the coniferous forest and you can enjoy a coffee halfway around at the café, which has an outside seating area. It's an ideal walk in hot weather as much of it is shaded by trees. There may be cyclists and horses on sections of this walk.

How to get there – From Chester follow the A51 signed for Nantwich, turning onto the A54 signed for Tarvin and Northwich. Shortly after the dual carriageway you will see Gresty's Waste car park on the right hand side of the road.

Grid Reference – SJ 539686

Postcode – CW6 0SP

Parking – Gresty's Waste car park

Facilities – There are toilets and a café at the half way point on the walk

You will need – Dog lead, poop bags and water for your dog in hot weather

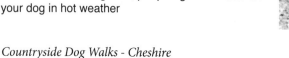

The Walk

1 Keep your dog on a lead to begin this walk. From the car park, face the road and take a path on the left hand side of the car park. Continue parallel with the road, and shortly after turn right, following the sign on the fingerpost for the Sandstone Trail. Cross the road with care. Take the path on the opposite side of the road, which is marked by a waymarker.

Pass a stone building on your left and a driveway for a house on your right. Pass beside a vehicle barrier and continue on the well-made track through the forest. Just after, ignore a narrow path on your right. On reaching a fingerpost, continue straight ahead following the sign for Delamere Forest.

You will begin to ascend gently. On reaching a track turn right, following the sign for Alternative Sandstone Trail Route. Pass an open area on your right, where you will begin to ascend on the surfaced path. Stay on the surfaced path, which bends sharply to your left, and ascend between fields. Continue on an elevated path, with young trees on your right.

Continue straight ahead. You will reach an open area on your right with aerial masts and trees on your left. Continue to ascend between fields. You will gain wonderful views as you continue.

2 You will reach a stone circle. Here each standing stone will indicate where all the shires are located. Brass plaques

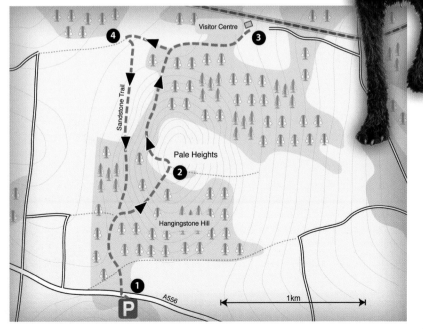

indicate where all the towns and villages are. There are fantastic views on a clear day. As you approach the stone circle, your continued path is on your left (just before reaching the stone circle). Descend and pass the stone marked Lancashire on your right. Continue on the surfaced path with a wire fence on your left and meadows on both sides.

Pass through a gap in the hedgerow and continue on the surfaced path. Trees are now on both sides of the track. You will begin to descend more steeply and you will have views ahead. When you pass the trees on your left, you will have wonderful views over the forest and across the fields beyond. Stay on the sealed path, which has a number of bends. When you see a car park ahead of you, put your dog on a lead, as there is an access road ahead for the car park. Pass beside a vehicle barrier and then turn right onto the access road. On reaching the wooden bollards, take the path on your left, which continues beside the track.

❸ You will reach the visitor centre, toilets and café on your left. On leaving the visitor centre, retrace your steps to the access road. Turn right on the path beside the access road. Pass the overflow car park on your left. Pass beside the wooden bollards on your left, and take a path on your right, immediately after.

Continue beside a picket fence on your right. There is a field on your far right. After you pass the fence, you will see a wet area in the forest on your far right, which can be very muddy, so you may want to keep your dog out. The path will bend to your right, and you will pass the field, which is replaced with woodland. Continue a little further until the path bends sharply to your right. Leave the path and continue straight ahead into the woods. Another path will become obvious as you continue. A little further along, turn a bend and descend on a sandy path. In the dip of the hill your dog will find water on your left. Ascend gently.

❹ On reaching a wide path, turn left where the path narrows, following the way marker for the Sandstone trail. The path undulates on the edge of woodland. A little further on there is a horse paddock on your left. At the end of the path, you will leave the wood and turn left on a track between fields. Keep your dog under close control, as this is an access track for vehicles. Shortly after, on reaching a junction for Eddisbury Lodge and a fingerpost, turn right following the sign for Nettleford Wood. Keep your dog under close control or on a lead, as this is an access track for a house and a farmyard.

Continue on the track, ascending gently between fields. Pass the farmyard and house on your left and continue ascending gently on the track between an avenue of trees. You will reach a farm gate and a kissing gate. Pass through the kissing gate and continue straight ahead. On reaching a track, cross it and continue straight ahead, where you are now on a familiar path.

Continue on the path. As you reach the fingerpost marked Stoney Lane, put your dog on a lead, as you will soon reach the busy main road. Cross the road with care and turn left on the path back to the car park.

14. Delamere *(Blakemere Moss)*   Easy - 3 miles - 2hrs

This forest walk is ideal for dogs, having very little road and no livestock. It has streams where your dog can get a drink and part of the walk follows beside a mere known as Blakemere Moss, where dogs can take a dip to cool off. The mere has many decaying tree stumps and often there are lots of gulls and wildfowl. There are some broadleaved trees amongst the coniferous forest. It's an ideal walk in hot weather. There may be cyclists and horses on sections of this walk.

How to get there – From Chester follow the A51 signed for Nantwich, turning onto the A54 for Tarvin and Northwich. Ignore the first brown sign for Delamere Forest. The road becomes the A556 as you pass the turn-off for Winsford on the right, at the fork in the road. On reaching the Vale Royal Abbey Arms pub on your right, turn left, following the brown sign for Delamere. Ignore the sign for Delamere visitor centre and train station and continue on the road a little further. You will see Whitefield car park on the right hand side of the road.

Grid Reference – SJ 556710   **Postcode** – CW8 2HZ

Parking – Whitefield car park

Facilities – There are no facilities

You will need – Dog lead, dog bags

The Walk

1 Keep your dog on a lead to begin this walk. From the car park, go back to the entrance and cross the road. Pass beside the vehicle barrier and continue straight ahead until you reach a wide path, just after. Cross the path and continue straight ahead, where you can view the mere. Retrace your steps back to the main path and turn right. Keep your dog under close control or on a lead, as the road runs parallel to the path to begin with and there are no boundary fences.

Pass a path on your left and continue straight ahead. You will now be at a safe distance from the road, so you can let your dog off the lead. Continue on the wide path with the mere on your right beyond the trees. You will pass beneath the 'Go Ape' high rope activity. A little further along you will pass paths on your left and right but continue straight ahead. You will lose sight of the mere now.

2 Your path will merge with another path on your left. Continue straight ahead. You will see a fingerpost signed for White Moor Gates/Station Road. Continue straight ahead here. On reaching a fork, take the path on your right. The area here is less shaded by trees. Ignore a path on your left. You can see the lake again on your right beyond the trees.

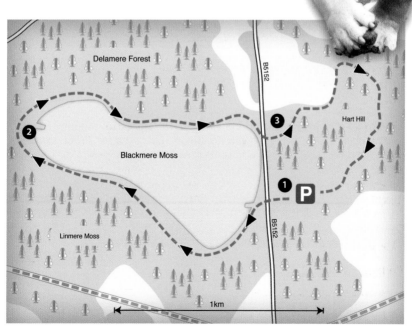

On reaching another path, turn right. Keep your dog under close control, or on a lead, as there is a road again on your left. You will pass a house over on your left on the road. Soon after, you will reach a vehicle barrier on your left. Put your dog on a lead and pass the vehicle barrier, where you will reach the road. Cross the road carefully and continue straight ahead on a narrow path into the wood.

❸ Ignore a path on your right just after, and ascend on the well-worn path. You will reach another path. Turn left and descend on the worn path between the trees and bracken. On reaching another path turn right. Continue beside a ditch on your left on the edge of the wood. Pass a wooden platform on your left. Cross a short boardwalk. Soon after you will reach a footbridge on your left. Don't go over the footbridge but turn right. You will pass a path on your left, almost immediately. A little further on, ignore a path on your right. Ascend slightly, where you will reach another path.

Turn right and again ascend gently. Pass some open areas on your left. Ignore a path on your left and continue straight ahead, where you will soon reach the car park.

15. The Kennels

Easy- 3 miles - 2hr

This circular walk is fairly level and you will follow on tracks, between two lakes which are fenced and screened off with hedgerows and scrub. A path will then connect onto the Whitegate Way, which is a disused railway line. You will have some views across the lake in places. There are some bridleways, so you may encounter horses. Some of the tracks are byways, so there is a possibility of traffic.

How to get there - From Chester follow the A51 signed for Nantwich, turning onto the A54 for Tarvin and Northwich. The road becomes the A556 as you pass the turn-off for Winsford on the right, at the fork in the road. Continue straight ahead at the next traffic lights, and just after you will pass Blakemere Village. Kennel Lane is the next turning on your right.

Grid Reference – SJ 599698   **Postcode** – CW8 2EA

Parking – Several lay-bys on Kennel Lane (Please keep clear of driveways and the residents only parking)

Facilities – There are no facilities

You will need – Dog leads, dog bags

The Walk

❶ Keep your dog on a lead to begin this walk. From the lay-by, continue heading further along the lane (in the opposite direction from the main road), where the road becomes a dirt track. Pass Foxhills Cottage on your left. You will reach and pass a bollard. Continue on the track. Towards the end of the track call your dog close, or put him on a lead. You will pass Kennel Cottage on your right, where you will reach an access road. Turn left on the road where just after, you will reach a sandy track (a byway).

❷ Continue on the track, with woods on your right and a paddock on your left. At the end of the paddock you begin to ascend gently on the track. You will pass a compound and a brick building on your right. On your far right there's a large pond. Continue between the hedges. A little further along, you will pass an open area and a vehicle barrier on your left. Just after, you will reach and continue beside a lake on your far left.

You will pass another vehicle barrier on your left, and then another on your right. Continue on the track, between hedges and scrub, now with lakes on both sides. As you continue you will pass another

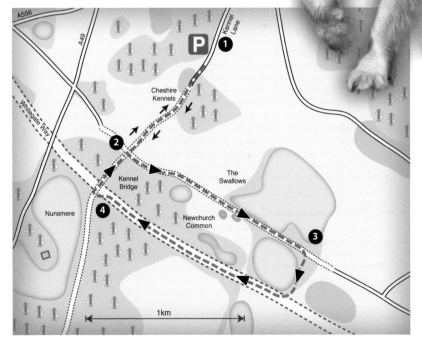

vehicle barrier on your right, and then on your left. Just after this vehicle barrier, pass a footpath on your left and then soon after, look for a footpath on your right.

❸ Take the footpath, and continue on the edge of young woodland. Soon after, you will reach a fork. Take the left path. You will reach and continue beside a chain link fence, with gardens beyond, and the lake is on your right. You will merge with a bridleway (another path) from your left and behind. After you pass the gardens there is a copse of trees on your left.

On reaching another path turn left. You will reach the Whitegate Way, which is a disused railway. Turn right onto the Whitegate Way, which is also a bridleway. Continue for some distance on this path. There is an option of using the narrow path on your right, which continues beside the disused railway. You will reach an old railway bridge.

❹ Take the path, which ascends to the bridge on your left. Cross the bridge known as Kennel Bridge, and continue on the sandy track. There is woodland on your left, and you will pass a scout camp on your right. After you pass the scout camp keep your dog under close control or on a lead, as there is an access road ahead.

On reaching the end of the track, pass beside a barrier, where you will reach an access road, and a familiar spot. Cross the access road and continue straight ahead. Retrace your steps, putting your dog on a lead on reaching the bollard. You will reach back to the road, where you have parked your car.

16. Brereton Heath Mere   Easy - 1.2 miles - 1hr

This is a lovely circular walk, where your dog can enjoy the water as you walk around the mere. You will cross on the edge of a large grass area, where your dog can run around, and then you will enter into broadleaved woodland, which is dominated by oak and silver birch.

How to get there – Brereton Heath can be found between Holmes Chapel and Congleton, off the A54. Look out for the sign to Brereton and turn onto Brereton Heath Lane, which is opposite Somerford Park Farm. You will find the car park on your left.

Grid Reference – SJ 794652

Postcode – CW12 4SU

Parking – Pay and display

Facilities – There are toilets and a visitor centre

You will need – Dog lead, dog bags

The Walk

❶ Leave the car park near to the pay and display. Turn left on a sealed path. Continue around the side of the visitor centre and toilet block. Keep your dog on a lead or under close control, as there is a road parallel on your right to begin with. Continue on the sealed path, with the mere on your far right. You will soon veer to your right, away from the road and close to the water's edge. Trees will screen your view across the mere in places.

Continue between the post and rail fences, with trees on both sides and pony paddocks beyond the trees on your left. You will reach a grass area on your left, and then a little further on you will pass a bird hide on your right. Immediately after reaching a wood on your left, take the worn path on your left, which isn't sealed. You will reach a fence corner on your right. Continue straight ahead, into the silver birch wood. Soon after, ignore a path on your right and continue straight ahead. Head towards a post and rail fence over on your left. Continue on the path beside the fence on your left.

❷ On reaching a kissing gate on your left, don't go through it, but turn right. Just after on reaching a fork take the path on your left. You will reach and continue beside a post and rail fence on your left. The

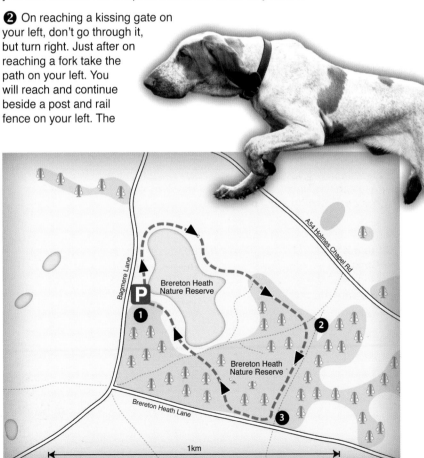

wood is predominantly oak and silver birch here. At the corner of the fence you will reach a kissing gate.

❸ Don't go through it, but turn right. Just after, at the fork turn left. Continue close to the road on the edge of the wood, and keep your dog on a lead or under close control, as the boundary is only a wire fence. Ignore any paths on your right.

On reaching a square post in the fence and a sign 'Advice to Motorists', turn right. Continue into the woods, leaving the road behind. Cross a footbridge over a ditch and continue straight ahead. Where the path forks, take the path on your left. Almost immediately turn left again. Pass a yellow butterfly on your left and shortly after pass a yellow marker post. Continue straight ahead, where you will pass another yellow marker over on your right (don't follow this marker post).

Continue straight ahead, where you will reach and continue beside a ditch on your left. You will soon reach a sealed path. Turn right just before the footbridge on your left, and continue on the sealed path. On reaching the mere again, turn left. Continue on a sealed path, having the lake over on your right. Continue on this path, where you will soon reach the car park.

17. Astbury Mere

Easy - 1.2 miles 1hr

This is a short but pleasant circular walk, with an option of extending it a little by ascending onto the edge of woodland, where you will have views across the mere. The path around the mere is mostly flat, and surfaced. The mere is screened off in places, by hedgerows and scrub. There is a very short section of road, where you will pass a boathouse. There are grass areas, where your dog can run around. There are no livestock on this walk, but there are wildfowl.

How to get there – Astbury Mere is located in Congleton. Take the A34, following the sign for Newcastle. Shortly after turn left onto Sandy Lane, following the brown sign for Astbury Mere Country Park. Continue on Sandy Lane, where you will reach the car park.

Grid Reference – SJ 845627

Postcode – CW12 4FR

Parking – There is a donation box in the car park

Facilities – There are toilets in the car park and a visitor centre

You will need – Dog lead, dog bags

The Walk

❶ From the car park, with your back to the visitor centre, take the path opposite, and a little over to your left. Pass a notice board, and go between the wooden barriers. Continue straight ahead, and then turn left on the surfaced path. Ignore a path on your right just after. Continue close to the mere on your right, which is beyond the hedges. There is a large grass area on your left.

Ignore a path which ascends, and continue around a right hand bend. You will reach a beach area on your right, where your dog can access the water. Here there is an option of extending your walk a little by ascending into the wood. There is a short section where you will walk close to a road if you choose the extension.

❷ For the extended walk choose A, and for the direct route go to B.

A. Now ascend the steps on the left of the path. On reaching another path turn right. Ascend another set of steps. Where the path begins to level out, take the path on your right and ascend the steps. On reaching a

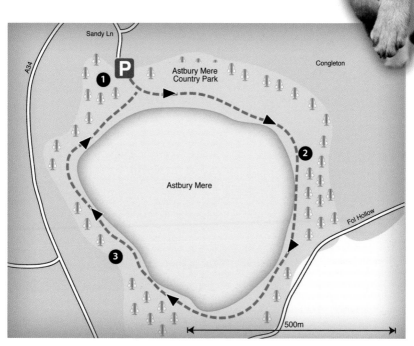

fingerpost turn right, following the sign for Fol Hollow. There is a field on your left and a hedge on your right. Pass between a low fence and then turn left on an elevated path.

There are views on your right across the mere. Continue on the path, with a wooded slope on your right. Ignore a path on your left, and put your dog on a lead or under close control, as you will walk beside a road on your left, with only a wire boundary fence. Take the next path on your right, and descend the steps. Veer left near to the bottom of the steps and then continue on the lakeside path, with the mere on your right.

B. Ignore the path on your left, with steps. Continue straight ahead, beside a grass bank on your left and the mere on your right. Ignore another path with steps on your left and continue straight ahead.

Both routes join here

Continue on the path and before reaching a post and rail fence on your left, put your dog on a lead. Pass beside a post with a car park on your left.

❸ Pass a boat club on your left and an open area, where you will have views across the mere. Continue on the quiet road in a pedestrian zone. You will soon leave the road and continue on a surfaced path beside the mere. There is a wooded bank on your left. The mere is fenced off for a while, preventing access for your dog. Continue on the path, where you will reach the large grass area once again. Take the path on your left, which will lead you back to the car park.

18. The Cloud

Med.-Chall. - 2.3 miles - 1hr 30min

This is a wonderful circular walk, where you will ascend through beautiful broadleaved woodland. There are fantastic panoramic views when you reach the top, where you will be surrounded by heathland, with some stone outcrops. There is a short section of road, but there are no livestock.

How to get there – Take junction 17 off the M6. Follow the sign for A534 Congleton. On reaching Congleton take the A54 signed for Buxton. After leaving the built up area, cross a canal bridge and then turn right on Middle Lane, following the brown sign for Picnic/Forest. Continue to follow the brown signs, where you will reach Timbersbrook picnic area and car park on your left.

Grid Reference – SJ 894627

Postcode – CW12 3PP

Parking – Free in the car park on Weathercock Lane

Facilities – There are no facilities

You will need – Dog lead, dog bags, water for your dog

The Walk

❶ From the car park, with your back to the entrance turn right and go to the furthest end of the car park. Pass through the barrier beside the gate and continue straight ahead on the gravel path. There is a grass area, which is surrounded by trees. Put your dog on a lead and ascend the steps, where you will reach a quiet road. Turn left and ascend the road, which has no pavement.

Pass a house on your right and soon after take the footpath on your right, which is signed on a fingerpost for Gritstone Trail. Ascend steeply on the path, which has some steps, through the mixed broadleaved wood. On reaching a fingerpost and another track turn right. Keep your dog on a lead or under close control, as there is vehicle access to a house ahead.

There is a bilberry and bracken covered wooded slope on your left. On reaching a bend there are views on your right over hilly countryside. Continue on the track between trees. Pass Folly Cottage on your right. Here you will see an exposed rock face on your left. Just after the cottage boundary fence, veer to your left and pass between squeeze posts to enter the National Trust site, known as The Cloud.

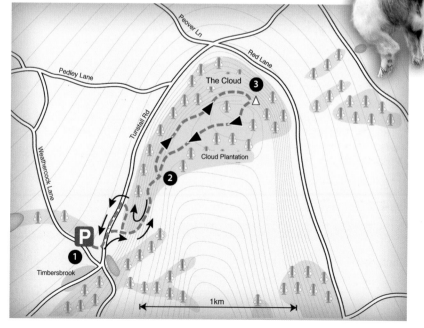

Ascend on the path through the wood, where in places there is exposed gritstone beneath your feet.

❷ On reaching another path turn left, following the waymarkers for Staffordshire Way. On reaching a clearing veer to your right, where another path joins from your left. Ascend gradually now. There is some heather and bilberry on your left, but the area is dominated by bracken and the woodland is silver birch and oak.

You will reach and pass beside a wooden barrier. Turn left and continue to ascend gradually through the wood. You will gain wonderful views on your left where the trees allow. The path will level out for a short while. Ascend gradually again on a narrow path between heather and bilberry, and regenerating silver birch.

The path will get steeper and bracken dominates the area. Ascend out of the tree line and continue beside the heather. You will pass some exposed stone on your left and then you will have panoramic views. Continue on the path between heather. The path will widen and you will head towards a larger outcrop of stone. Pass the outcrop on your left, and continue straight ahead, where you will reach a trig point and a topograph.

❸ Before you reach the trig point, your return path is the first path on your right. After you have enjoyed the views, descend on the path between bracken and heather, heading towards woodland. As you reach the edge of the wood, veer to your right on the path. You will descend through the wood on a wide path.

You will reach a familiar spot. Pass beside the wooden barrier, and retrace your steps through the wood on the wide path. Turn right and follow the waymarker for Staffordshire Way. Descend and pass Folly Cottage. Pass a fingerpost and a path on your left and continue on the access road. Keep your dog under close control or on a lead, as you will reach the quiet road.

On reaching the road turn left and descend. A little further along, pass a fingerpost on your left from your outbound route, and one on your right. Just after you pass Ivy Cottage on your right, take the path on your right and continue to the car park.

19. Raw Head

Med - 1.9 miles - 1hr 30min

This circular walk takes you to the highest point on the Sandstone Trail, which is a long distance path. There are views on reaching a trig point, and you will see sandstone outcrops amongst wonderful broadleaved woodland. You will descend and then return on the edge of farmland on a farm track. There may be livestock for part of this walk but there are no roads, except for an access road.

How to get there – From Chester, take the A41 in the direction of Whitchurch. At the Broxton roundabout turn left onto the A534, following the sign for Nantwich. You will pass a crossroad and sign for Bickerton, Egerton Green and Cholmondeley on your right. A little further along the road (after passing two more lanes on your left) you will see Coppermines Lane on your left. Take this and continue to the end of the lane.

Grid Reference – SJ 520550   **Postcode** – SY14 8BY

Parking – Free at the end of Coppermines Lane (at a junction of lanes)

Facilities – There are no facilities

You will need – Dog lead, dog bags and water for your dog in hot weather

The Walk

❶ Face the interpretation panel for the Sandstone Trail and turn left. Continue on a track between fields, keeping your dog under close control or on a lead, as there may be vehicles accessing a farm ahead. You will have views on your right. Pass 'The Bungalow' on your right and then leave the track, which bends to your left. Continue straight ahead, following the sign for Rawhead.

You will see a waymarker. Turn left here and pass through a kissing gate. Continue on the path between trees. Ignore a path on your right, marked by a waymarker and continue straight ahead. You will pass a rock face on your left. Continue on the path, which cuts across a woodland slope. Ascend steps in places. There are ferns on the woodland floor, and you will pass another section of rock face. The path is undulating and you will reach and continue beside a field with a wire fence on your left.

You will pass a set of steps on your right. A little further along, ignore another dilapidated set of steps on your right. Keep your dog on a lead or under close control as there are a couple of sheer faces ahead on your right. Just after, ascend the sandstone steps and continue beside a wire fence. You will have wonderful views on your right and left at this spot.

Continue on the path, which has steeply sloped woodland on your right. Descend and pass a fingerpost and path on your right, signed for Harthill Village. Continue straight ahead, where you will reach a trig point at Rawhead.

❷ This is the highest point on the Sandstone Trail. Now retrace your steps until you reach the fingerpost, signed for Harthill Village. Turn left here, and descend the steps. Continue on the woodland path which cuts through the hillside, descending quite steeply in places.

On reaching a road turn right. Continue on an access track, keeping your dog under close control or on a lead. Pass a wooden storage unit, where you will leave the access road. Continue straight ahead on a grass track.

Pass through a farm gate straight ahead, and continue on the edge of a field. The track will split into two. Keep to your right, and continue on the track. Ignore the stile on your right and continue straight ahead, where you will pass through another farm gate.

Continue straight ahead, where you will reach a familiar spot. Now retrace you steps back to Coppermines Lane where you have parked your car.

20. Beeston

Med.-Chall. - 3 miles - 2hr

This is an amazing circular walk, which starts from Beeston Castle. You will pass through wonderful broadleaved woodland where you will ascend a wooded hill, which can be a little steep in parts. There are views of two castles: Peckforton and Beeston. You will go through farmland, some of which is arable, but there is a short section of the walk where you may be amongst cattle. There is a country lane which connects between woodland and farmland.

How to get there – If you are coming from Chester, take the A51 signed for Nantwich, and on reaching Tarporley follow the brown signs for Beeston Castle.

Grid Reference – SJ 539590 **Postcode** - CW6 9TX

Parking – Pay and display in the Beeston Castle car park

Facilities – There are no facilities unless you pay to enter Beeston Castle. Dogs are allowed on a lead

You will need – Dog lead, dog bags and water in hot weather

The Walk

❶ From the car park, go out onto the road and turn left. Continue beside the castle outer wall on your right. Soon after, leave the road as it bends to your left and continue straight ahead, following the sign on the fingerpost for Sandstone Trail/Whitchurch. Continue beside the wall on your right and a hedgerow on your left.

On reaching the pine wood, continue for about 30 yards on the woodland edge, beside a stock fence on your left. Look out for a slightly worn path on your right, which continues through the wood. Take this path and continue diagonally through the wood, descending on the slope. Keep your dog under close control or on a lead, as there is a road ahead.

Pass through a barrier and turn left on the road. Just after, take the footpath on your right. Ascend the steps and pass through a kissing gate. Keep your dog under close control and cross through the middle of the field on the obvious path. You will see Peckforton Castle in the distance ahead. On reaching the end of the field, pass through the kissing gate. Descend the steps and cross a footbridge over a stream. Dogs can get water here.

Ascend the steps and continue straight ahead, where you will

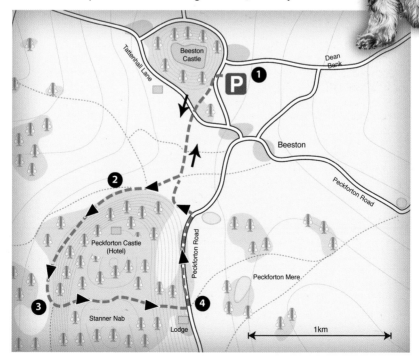

continue on the edge on an arable field, with a hedgerow on your right. Keep your dog on the path, to avoid any damage to crops and during the nesting season there may be ground nesting birds. Turn right where you see the fingerpost, following the sign for Sandstone Trail. Keep your dog under close control as there may be cattle grazing here. Pass through the kissing gate and cross through the middle of the field on the obvious path.

At the end of the field pass through the kissing gate and turn right on the quiet access track. Keep your dog under close control or on a lead, as there may be traffic and there are houses. Pass some houses on your right, and in places you will have views of Beeston Castle on your right. On reaching a fingerpost at the entrance for Peckforton Estate, put your dog on a lead.

2 Pass through the gate and continue on the track through mixed broadleaved woods. There are pheasants being reared in this area. The track is also a bridleway, therefore you may encounter horses.

You will begin to ascend and gain some views on your right. Continue for quite a distance. Pass through a gateway, where you will see a fingerpost.

3 Leave the track here, and turn left on a path which isn't marked. Ascend gently through the woods on a dirt path. As the ascent steepens there are some steps. On reaching a track turn left, and descend gradually. Soon after, before a gate, turn right on a path, which is waymarked. Continue on a fairly level path through the wood.

You will soon descend gradually. Pass a large boulder over on your right. Soon after you will veer to your left. The path becomes slightly sunken, and there are bramble banks on either side. After the short sunken section of the path put your dog on a lead, or under close control as there is a road ahead. On reaching the road, turn right. Pass beside a vehicle barrier and continue straight ahead. Go through the arch of the gatehouse, where you will reach a road.

4 Turn left on the road, taking care as there are no pavements. You will pass Ivy Cottage on your left. When you reach another house on your left, turn left immediately after on the private road. You will see Beeston Castle in the distance on your right.

When you see a fingerpost on your right signed for Beeston Castle, go through the kissing gate. Keep your dog on the path to avoid any damage to crops and continue straight ahead, on the edge of the field. You will have views straight ahead of Beeston Castle. On reaching a fingerpost and kissing gate on your left you will be in a familiar spot. Ignore the path on your left and continue straight ahead, where you will retrace your steps.

At the end of the field continue straight ahead and cross the footbridge. Continue straight ahead through another field. Turn left on the road and soon after turn right and enter back into the wood. Continue on the path, which ascends through the wood and veer to your left. Put your dog on a lead, or under close control and continue on the path beside the castle wall, where you will soon reach the road and car park.

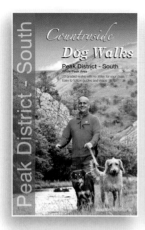

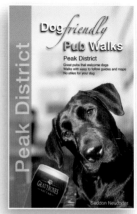

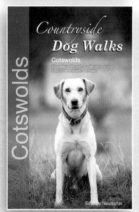

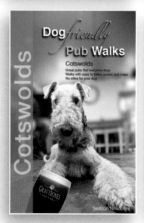

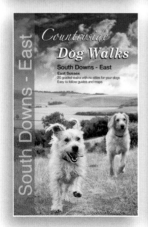

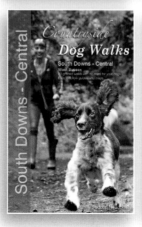

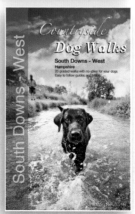

www.countrysidedogwalks.co.uk

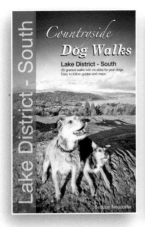
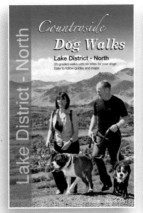
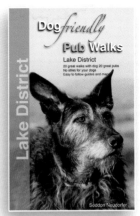
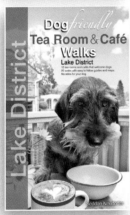
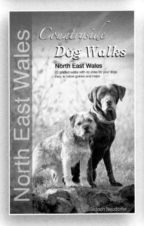
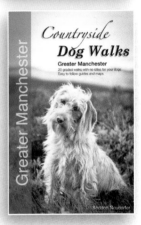
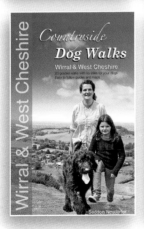
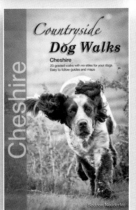
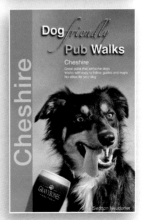

New Release Nov - 2016

Simple recipes made from ingredients in your kitchen

Healthy ingredients to ensure a healthy dog

Fun and easy to make

Wet Nose Publishing Ltd

"Cooking treats is easy"